TRIBES of NATIVE AMERICA

Menominee

edited by Marla Felkins Ryan
and Linda Schmittroth

**BLACKBIRCH®
PRESS**

THOMSON

GALE

San Diego • Detroit • New York • San Francisco • Cleveland
New Haven, Conn. • Waterville, Maine • London • Munich

THOMSON

GALE

Photo credits: Cover Courtesy of Northwestern University Library; cover © National Archives; cover © Photospin; cover © Perry Jasper Photography; cover © Picturequest; cover © Seattle Post-Intelligencer Collection, Museum of History & Industry; cover © PhotoDisc; cover © Library of Congress; page 5 © Wisconsin Historical Society, by Prat, ID: 6049; page 6 © Joseph Sohm/ChromoSohm Inc./CORBIS; page 8 © Wisconsin Historical Society, by Edwin Willard Deming, ID: Whi-1870; pages 9, 10, 22, 24 © Nancy Carter/North Wind Picture Archive; page 11 © Wisconsin Historical Society, by Edwin Willard Deming, ID: 1900; page 12 © Smithsonian American Art Musem, Washington DC/Art Resource, NY; page 13 © Library of Congress; page 14, 19, 20 © CORBIS; page 15 © Bettmann/CORBIS; page 17 © Wisconsin Historical Society, WHi(X3) 18851; page 18 © Wisconsin Historical Society, ID: 1868; page 21 © Milwaukee Public Museum; page 23 © Wisconsin Historical Society, WHi(X3) 26184; page 26 © COREL; page 27 © AP Photo/Shawano Leader; page 29 © Minnesota Histrical Society; page 31 © AP Photo/The Capital Times, David Sandell; page 32 © Hulton|Archive/Getty Images; page 33 © Wisconsin Historical Society, by Samuel Marsden Brookes, ID: 1888

LIBRARY OF CONGRESS CATALOGING-IN-PUBLICATION DATA

Menominee / Marla Felkins Ryan, book editor ; Linda Schmittroth, book editor.
    v. cm. — (Tribes of Native America)
Includes bibliographical references and index.
Contents: Name — History — Government — Daily life — Current tribal issues.
  ISBN 1-56711-697-3 (alk. paper)
  1. Menominee Indians—History—Juvenile literature. 2. Menominee Indians—Social life and customs—Juvenile literature. [1. Menominee Indians. 2. Indians of North America—Michigan. 3. Indians of North America—Wisconsin.] I. Ryan, Marla Felkins. II. Schmittroth, Linda. III. Series.

  E99.M44M45 2003
  977.4004'973--dc21

                                                                2003002630

Table of Contents

MENOMINEE

Name

Menominee (pronounced *muh-NOM-uh-nee*) means "wild rice people." The Menominee had this name because wild rice was a large part of their diet.

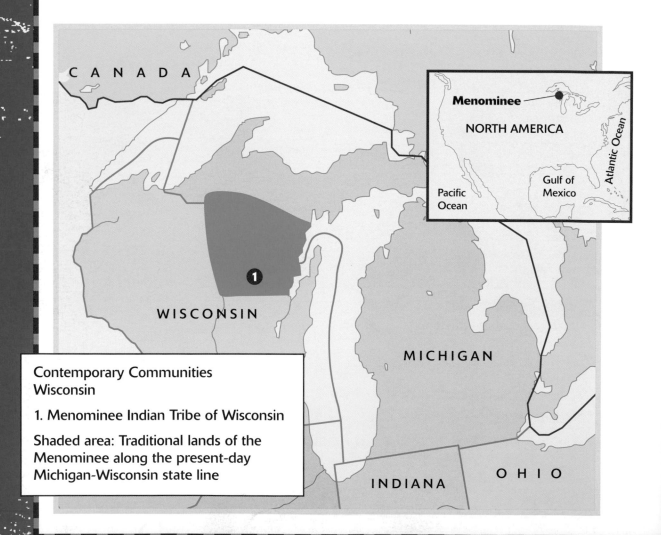

CANADA

WISCONSIN

MICHIGAN

INDIANA

OHIO

Menominee

NORTH AMERICA

Pacific Ocean

Gulf of Mexico

Atlantic Ocean

Contemporary Communities
Wisconsin

1. Menominee Indian Tribe of Wisconsin

Shaded area: Traditional lands of the Menominee along the present-day Michigan-Wisconsin state line

Where are the traditional Menominee lands?

The Menominee live on the Wisconsin Reservation. It is 45 miles northwest of the city of Green Bay. The reservation covers about 235,000 acres. Most of the reservation has thick forests. The reservation has two large villages called Neopit and Keshena.

The Menominee have inhabited the area that includes what is now Wisconsin for thousands of years.

The Menominee once controlled vast areas of land around the Wisconsin River (pictured).

Origins and group ties

For the past five thousand years, the Menominee have lived in present-day Michigan and Wisconsin. The tribe says it first lived near Sault (pronounced SOO) Sainte Marie in Michigan's Upper Peninsula. Around 1400, the tribe was forced to move westward by the Potawatomi and Ojibway. Together with the Winnebago and Ojibway, the Menominee are one of the original tribes of Wisconsin and parts of Michigan.

What has happened to the population?

In 1634, there were between 2,000 and 4,000 Menominee. By 1768, the number had dropped to 800. In 1854, the number was up to 1,930. In 1956, there were 2,917 Menominee. In a 1990 population count by the U.S. Bureau of the Census, 8,064 people.

At one time, the Menominee ruled over nearly 10 million acres. Their lands stretched from the Great Lakes to the Mississippi River. They were hunter-gatherers. Sometimes, they also fished. The Menominee were a brave and generous tribe. They lived peacefully among larger and more powerful tribes. Their lives changed as American settlers and loggers took more and more Menominee land. After 1856, the tribe was forced onto a reservation.

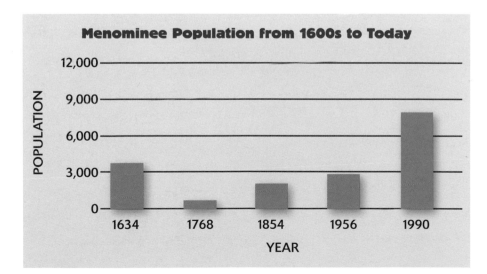

Menominee Population from 1600s to Today

HISTORY

French upset peaceful existence

The Menominee have lived on their tribal lands for at least five thousand years. This is the longest of any Wisconsin tribe. In 1634, Frenchman Jean Nicolet (pronounced *JHON Nik-o-LAY*) passed through Menominee territory. He was the first European to make contact with the tribe. Nicolet thought he could find a pathway to China. Over the next thirty years, the Menominee had little contact with the French traders who came after Nicolet. Because of the fur trade, though, they

This painting shows the 1634 arrival of Jean Nicolet, the first European to meet the Menominee.

The Menominee traded furs to the French for a variety of items, including metal cookware like the iron pots pictured here.

suffered at the hands of other tribes who traded with the French.

The fur trade in Canada and around the Great Lakes caused strong rivalries among native tribes. Eager to trade furs for French goods, some hunters began to hunt on the lands of neighboring tribes. Stronger tribes forced weaker ones to move westward. Refugees from the Ojibway and Potawatomi tribes crowded onto Menominee lands. Wars broke out among tribes as Indians competed for food and land. Many people starved to death. Others died from warfare and illness.

Trading post built

In 1667, the French built a trading post at Green Bay, Wisconsin. By this time, there were fewer than four hundred Menominee left. These Native Americans had become dependent on the fur

1909–1930
Tribal sawmill provides jobs, but tribe must fight to manage the mill

1917–1918
WWI is fought in Europe

1929
Stock market crash begins the Great Depression

1941
Bombing at Pearl Harbor forces United States into WWII

1945
WWII ends

1950s
Reservations are no longer controlled by federal government

1954
Menominee federal tribal status is ended. It is restored in 1973

1989–1990
The National Museum of the American Indian Act and the Native American Grave Protection and Reparations Act bring about the return of burial remains to native tribes

The Menominee traded animal hides, like the one shown on this stretching rack, with the French. The tribe benefited from the fur trade until 1696.

trade. They traded with the French for goods such as metal kettles, steel tools, cloth, needles, and scissors. Trade changed forever the Menominee's ancient way of life. At one time, they hunted only for what they needed. Trade turned them into a tribe that hunted for profit. But trade may also have saved the tribe from dying out. The French kept the peace among rival tribes to protect trade. The Menominee were saved from more warfare. Because so many tribes trapped furs, soon there were more furs than the French needed. The French ended trade in the area in 1696.

Tribe joins in white men's wars

The Menominee began to hunt, fish, and gather crops again. Life was no longer peaceful for the tribe. Throughout the 1700s, they found themselves caught up in warfare over and over again. This time the conflict was among French, British, and American colonists. The different groups fought to dominate North America. When they could not avoid conflict, the Menominee sided with the French. The Menominee liked the French because they had never tried to take over native lands. After the French were defeated in the French and Indian War (1756-1763),

The Menominee joined forces with the French and later the British when their countries fought American colonists.

the Menominee became allies of the British. They fought with the British against the colonists in the American Revolutionary War (1775–1783). They also sided with the British in the War of 1812. This war was between the United States and Britain.

At last, the Menominee befriended the Americans. In 1815, Americans built a fort at Green Bay. Soon a trading post was opened at the Menominee village of Minikani.

Menominee warriors, like the one in this portrait, fought to keep tribal lands.

A time of treaties

Americans wanted land. Greatly outnumbered, the Menominee were forced to give up more and more of their land. The Menominee did not always give up their lands peacefully. Between 1817 and 1856, the Menominee made eight treaties with the United States. A treaty signed in 1831 gave the tribe eight cents an acre for 3 million acres of wooded land. By 1850, nearly all tribal lands were owned by whites. The Menominee fought, but the pressure was too great. The Wolf Treaty of 1854 created a reservation for them in northern Wisconsin.

Loggers come

The Menominee tribe sent 125 men to the Union army during the American Civil War (1861–1965). This was a large number of warriors for a tribe that had only about 2000 members. Menominee warriors fought at the Civil War battles of Vicksburg and Petersburg. Menominee guarded the people who plotted to assassinate President Abraham Lincoln during their trial and execution.

American loggers were unable to take Menominee lands.

After the Civil War, American loggers went to Wisconsin. They wanted to cut down trees and sell the timber. They knew the forests could make them rich. The loggers tried every means they could think of—legal and illegal—to take Menominee lands. The loggers failed.

By 1870, the Menominee had built three villages along the Menominee River. They built another eight villages to the south. The Menominee fought the government's efforts to turn them into farmers. They chose instead to make money by logging.

Logging success nearly destroys tribe

The Menominee were very successful in their logging business. By 1890, the tribe had built a hospital and school. They also set up their own police and court systems. At this time, most other Native American tribes struggled to adjust to reservation life. The Menominee tribe was looked upon as a model of prosperity and modern thinking. The tribe's success nearly led to their destruction. Their troubles began in the 1950s when the U.S. Congress adopted a policy called termination.

Logging brought prosperity to the Menominee in the late nineteenth century.

This photo shows Menominee and their supporters at a protest of the U.S. government's termination policy.

Termination was part of a larger U.S. plan to make Indians more like white Americans. Termination ended special government funds and programs for Indian tribes. For the first time, the tribe had to pay state taxes. The effect of termination on the Menominee was very bad. Many Menominee were unable to pay their taxes, and lost their land. The Menominee were soon among the poorest people in the state of Wisconsin.

Anger over termination grew. In 1970, the Menominee formed a protest movement called the Determination of Rights and Unity for Menominee Shareholders (DRUMS). They used protest marches and legal actions to slow the sale of tribal lands. In 1973, President Richard Nixon signed the Menominee Restoration Act. This act gave back tribal status to the reservation.

Religion

The Menominee believed in a Great Spirit. This spirit made the sun, the stars, and the earth. They believed in other spirits who took the form of animals. In the Menominee creation story, one of those spirits was named Great Bear. He asked the Great Spirit to transform him into a man. His wish was granted. Great Bear soon felt lonely. He asked a golden eagle to become his brother. The eagle became known as Thunderer. Great Bear then asked a beaver to join him. She became Beaver Woman. This small family adopted other spirits. The animal spirits who became people were the first Menominee.

A MODEL COMMUNITY FAILS

In the 1800s, reformers wanted to convert the Menominee to Christianity. They wanted the tribe to act more like European Americans. In 1831, the reformers built a community called Winnebago Rapids. The town had twelve houses, a school, a farm, a blacksmith shop, and a sawmill. The town was an experiment in peaceful living through education and good example. It was a total failure. The Menominee did not like the model homes. Some used the homes as stables for their horses. They tore up the floorboards for firewood. The Indians slept in their own traditional shelters pitched nearby. They refused to listen to the lessons of the teachers and preachers.

The Menominee had a religious society called the Medicine Lodge Religion. Its main purpose was to make life last longer. The society taught proper behavior. It also taught members how to use plants and herbs to heal the sick. The Menominee also took part in the Drum (or Dream) Dance Religion. The religion taught that dreams make people sick when they are not acted out.

Today, most Menominee are Roman Catholic. Some Menominee in rural areas belong to the Native American Church. The church combines Christian and Native American beliefs and practices.

Followers of the Menominee Drum Dance Religion used decorated drums, like the one in this photo, in their ceremonies.

Government

In the early days, the Menominee had a tribal council that ruled informally. When native refugees from the fur-trade wars arrived on Menominee lands, they threatened the Menominee way of life. The tribe needed a stronger form of government. The tribal council was made up of elders from each clan. It picked a chief to lead the tribe in war with the refugees. Later, the job of the chief grew. He kept the peace, approved tribal policies, and led ceremonies. In general, he looked out for the good of his people.

Menominee chiefs led the tribe in times of both peace and war.

When the Menominee reservation was created in 1854, the tribe had to obey U.S. laws. In the 1950s, the U.S. government put tribal government under the control of the state of Wisconsin. Menominee reservation lands became a county of Wisconsin.

In 1973, the Menominee Restoration Act was signed. This act reestablished the tribe's reservation. In 1977, the tribe adopted a constitution. In 1979, a tribal legislature was formed.

Economy

Before the Europeans arrived, the Menominee hunted wild animals for food. They also gathered the plentiful wild rice on their lands. They believed that to plant crops rather than gather rice might offend the Creator.

Reformers in the 1800s tried to turn the Menominee into farmers. The Menominee chose instead to sell the wood from pine trees to make money. In 1909, the U.S. government gave the Menominee a sawmill. The mill gave jobs to everyone in the tribe. The government did not give management of the mill to the tribe.

The U.S. government provided a sawmill (pictured) to the Menominee, but did not allow them to run it themselves.

Economy based on forests

In 1930, the Menominee sued for greater tribal management of the mill. Thirteen lawsuits were filed, but the Menominee did not get what they wanted from the courts. Meanwhile, more than two hundred Menominee served in World War II (1939–1945). Back home, women worked at the tribal sawmill. In 1954, the U.S. government ended the Menominee's tribal status. The 2,917 Menominee became very poor. They were forced to sell their lands to white developers. Angry Menominee united behind the organization called Determination of Rights and Unity for Menominee Shareholders (DRUMS). By 1973, they regained their federal tribal status. The tribe began to log again.

Despite thirteen lawsuits, the Menominee could not gain management of their sawmill.

The Menominee use good forest management practices. For every tree cut down for timber, the Menominee plant a new one in its place. Their forestlands grew by 10 percent in the twentieth century.

Recently, the tribe opened gambling centers to create much-needed jobs. Unemployment is high on the reservation. Nearly 22 percent of the Menominee tribe does not have a job. Most Menominee adults earn only about $4,700 a year.

DAILY LIFE

Games

Because the Menominee did not need to work hard to find food, they had time for fun. Lacrosse, a game invented by Native Americans, was a favorite pastime for Menominee men. It is played on a field by two teams of ten players each. Each player has a long-handled stick with a webbed pouch. A player uses this stick to get a ball into the opposing team's goal.

Children played with dolls, bows and arrows, and hoops made of tree bark. In the winter, families gathered around the fire to listen to stories.

A favorite pastime of the Menominee, lacrosse is played using a stick with a webbed pouch and a ball.

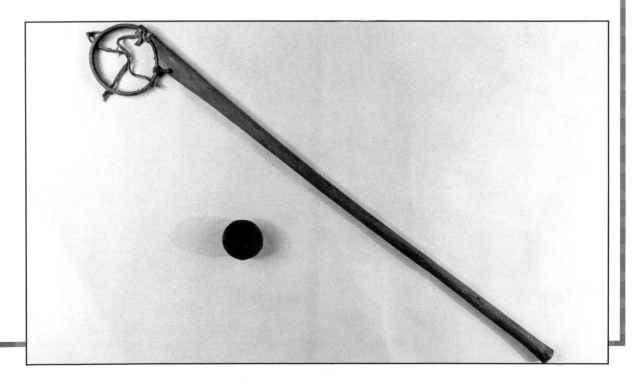

Layers of tree bark cover this dome-shaped Menominee wigwam.

Buildings

In the summer, the Menominee lived in large villages. They built dome-shaped wigwams. A frame made of young trees was covered with mats of woven tree bark. Inside, mats made from long, flat leaves gave warmth and protection from the rain. The mats were sometimes colored with dyes made from fruits and berries. Animal skins or grass mats were placed on the ground or on raised sleeping platforms. The Menominee liked to cook and eat outside.

In the winter, smaller groups of extended families went back to their hunting grounds. They built dome-shaped wigwams that were similar to their summer homes. They also built sweat lodges to purify their bodies and to cure diseases. There was also a home for the medicine man.

As late as the 1950s, a few elderly Menominee still lived in bark houses. Today, most Menominee live in homes no different from non–Native Americans. The only difference is that Menominee put small totem poles outside their front doors.

Clothing

The early Menominee wore little clothing in warm weather. In cool weather, they wore buckskin breechcloths. These garments had front and back flaps that hung from the waist. They also wore leggings and moccasins. They wore cloaks for formal occasions. In the winter, snowshoes made travel easier. Sometimes, the Menominee painted their skin.

A mother and child wear traditional Menominee clothing, decorated with ribbon and porcupine quills.

The Menominee decorated their clothing with great skill. They used satin ribbon and porcupine quills to create special shapes. Popular patterns were diamonds, leaves, deer heads, and thunderbirds.

In the nineteenth century, Menominee women began to wear full skirts like their white neighbors. Although they dressed like white women, they also wore turquoise and silver or beaded jewelry. At the turn of the twentieth century, fashionable men wore cotton shirts with ruffles, silk ribbons, and fancy pins.

Food

The name Menominee means "wild rice people." Wild rice is a cereal grass that grows in lakes and streams. The Menominee used canoes to harvest the wild rice. Menominee women stood in the canoe to reach for the tall, hollow rice stalks. They held the stalks over the boat and shook them. The wild rice fell into the canoe. The wild rice was boiled and often flavored with maple syrup.

Menominee women gathered wild rice (pictured), nuts, and fruit as part of the tribe's healthful diet.

Women also gathered nuts, fruits, and berries. Menominee men hunted ducks and geese to add to the tribe's diet. They caught fish with spears and nets. The tribe ate a healthful, well-balanced diet. Early explorers commented on the good health of the Menominee people.

In the nineteenth century, some Menominee began to farm. They grew potatoes, beans, oats, corn, melons, and fruit trees. They also bred hogs. Farmers and wild-rice gatherers often shared their harvests.

Healing practices

The Menominee believed that supernatural powers and evil witches caused illness. When a member of the tribe became ill, a medicine man called a shaman (pronounced *SHAH-mun or SHAY-mun*) was asked to help. He brought a bag of cures to the sick person's home. His bag might have healing roots and herbs, charms such as deer tails, or carved wooden puppets. He also had a medicine stick to use as an offering to the spirits.

The Menominee had many herbal medicines. They used the different parts of a tree to make cures for swellings, sores, and colds. The Menominee used mint for pneumonia. They had herbal medicines for poison ivy, childbirth, stomachaches, sleeplessness, and lung trouble. Bug repellants and painkillers were

The Menominee made many medicines from herbs. They used mint (above) to treat pneumonia.

very important. An herb called Seneca snakeroot was a popular medicine. The Menominee picked so much of it that the plant nearly became extinct.

Menominee warriors fought in the French and Indian War (1756–1763). After the war, they brought smallpox back to their villages. More than one-fourth of the Menominee tribe died from this illness. In the 1830s, U.S. soldiers carried smallpox and cholera into Wisconsin. Another 25 percent of the Menominee population died. The natives had no natural defense against the diseases.

Education

Menominee children learned by example. Soon after the tribe moved to the reservation in 1854, the Menominee built a school. They lost it when a 1954 law ended the reservation.

With the profits from their timber business, the Menominee built a college and four reservation schools. More than five hundred children attend the reservation's schools. The College of the Menominee Nation teaches forestry, health care, and gambling administration.

Two students of the College of the Menominee Nation proudly wear full tribal dress.

CUSTOMS

Clan structure and rituals

The Menominee are divided into groups called Bear and Thunderer. (These two figures played a large part in the tribe's creation story.) Each group is made up of clans whose members consider one another brothers and sisters. Membership is passed down through the father. The Bear symbol is a female bear with a long tail. An eagle is the symbol of Thunderer.

Today's Menominee keep some of their ancient rites. For example, tobacco offerings are left at a stone called Spirit Rock to please the hero Manabozho. He turned a greedy warrior to stone for the request of eternal life. Menominee legend states that when Spirit Rock crumbles away, the Menominee will perish.

Festivals

Long ago, the Menominee held a Beggars' Dance in the fall. The dance celebrated the maple syrup season. Each year, modern Menominee have two festivals. The Veterans Powwow takes place in the spring. The Annual Menominee Nation Contest Powwow takes place in the summer. At these

The Menominee and other tribes gather twice each year for powwows like the one in this photo.

powwows, members of several different tribes come together for dance contests and tribal drumming performances.

Hunting and gathering rituals

Before they gathered wild rice, the Menominee threw tobacco onto the water to please the spirits. (Tobacco was thought to be sacred.) When they set off to hunt, they took only a small amount of food, along with their clothing and sleeping mats. They hunted with bows that were coated with bear grease. Their arrows were made of pine or cedar wood. Bear was a favorite prey. When a bear was killed, a special ceremony and feast was held. All the hunter's friends were invited.

A Native American burial mound lies in the middle of a forest.

Burial

The dead were buried in the ground. A spirit house marked the grave. Some Menominee still follow this burial custom.

Current tribal issues

The Menominee often fight with sportsmen and groups that want to protect the environment over how the tribe uses its ancestral lands. Some groups claim Native Americans should not be able to use modern methods when they fish. Others claim that the Menominee have already given up their fishing

Menominee leaders like Lisa Waukau (second from right) actively participate in decisions regarding land rights.

rights. There is more at stake than how the Menominee catch their fish. The Menominee economy is partly based on fishing.

Menominee leaders are concerned about their environment. They objected to the storage of nuclear waste on the reservation. They fought against plans for a copper mine that could have polluted the Wolf River.

Menominee leader Ada Deer.

Notable People

Ada Deer (1935–) is a lifelong advocate for social justice. She helped to create Determination of Rights and Unity for Menominee Shareholders (DRUMS). She was the first woman to head the U.S. Bureau of Indian Affairs.

Tribal leader Oshkosh (1795–1858), also known as Claw, promoted peace with white settlers. Despite his best efforts, Menominee lands were taken over. He was forced to move his people to a reservation that was only a tiny size of the tribe's former homeland.

For More Information

Ourada, Patricia K. *The Menominee*. New York: Chelsea House, 1990.

Paterek, Josephine. *Encyclopedia of American Indian Costume*. New York: W.W. Norton, 1994.

Sultzman, Lee. **Menominee History**. (www.dickshovel.com/men.html).

Oshkosh, a tribal leader, tried unsuccessfully to protect Menominee lands.

Glossary

Drum (or Dream) Dance Religion a Native American religion that taught people to act out their dreams

Lacrosse a Native American game played with a ball and long poles with webbed pouches

Medicine Lodge Religion a Menominee religion intended to make life longer

Powwow a Native American gathering or ceremony

Reservation land set aside for Native Americans by the government

Shaman a Native American priest who used magic to heal people and see the future

Treaty an agreement between two or more parties

Wigwam a Native American hut made of bark and hides

Index